DESERTS

Angela Wilkes

Illustrated by Peter Dennis

Revised by
Felicity Brooks and Stephen Wright

Contents

Consultant: Dr. Andrew Warren
University College London

In the Desert

Deserts are the driest places in the world. In parts of them, it may not rain for many years.

Most deserts are very hot in the daytime, but they cool off at night and can be very cold.

When it rains, sand and stones are carried down from the hills by floodwater and left in fan-shaped patterns on the ground.

Most deserts are rocky and bare. Parts of them are covered in sand. When the wind blows, the sand piles up into small hills called dunes.

Few plants and animals can live in the desert because it is too dry. The ones that are there all have ways of living without much water.

is plain floods after rain, the rain soon dries up in the hot sun, leaving behind patches of salt.

In parts of deserts, there are big, strange rocks. They may be all that is left of a mountain.

Caravan of camels taking salt across the desert

Patch of salt

Where there is water, it may make an oasis – a place where trees and plants can grow.

Although it is hard to find water and food in the desert, some people live there. Many of them are nomads. They move around from place to place and set up their camps wherever they can find a well or a waterhole.

How the Desert Changes

The wind does strange things in the desert. It whips up spiraling columns of dust.

The wind blows the sand so that it moves and changes direction like ripples on water.

If there is something in the sand's way, such as grass, the sand piles up behind it.

Dunes

The moving sand usually piles up to make a small dune. Sand blows up one side of a dune then slides down the other side, which is steeper.

The dune grows larger and moves forward very slowly. The sand around dunes is soft and vehicles can easily get stuck in it.

There was once a river in this desert. It made this channel thousands of years ago.

It washed broken rocks down from the hills. They now lie on the plains below.

Desert rocks slowly change all the time. Wind-blown sand wears them into odd shapes.

Sometimes just part of the rock wears away. This natural rock arch is in the state of Utah.

Many rocks are jagged. Sudden rain, heat or cold cracks them and then pieces break off.

These spiky rock towers in Bryce Canyon in Utah, were once part of an area of high, flat land.

A Storm in the Arizona Desert

Big trees have very long roots to help them find water.

Saguaro cactus

This ocotillo bush has dropped its leaves so that it does not need so much water.

Many trees and bushes grow near dried-up streams, where water may be stored below the ground.

Sandy stream-bed

Prickly pear cactus

Everything that grows in the desert needs water. It has not rained here for many months and the ground is hard, dry and dusty.

The plants look dead, but they are alive. They all have ways of surviving in the dry season. Then when it rains, they grow and flower.

There are sometimes huge thunder-storms in parts of the desert. Then there is heavy rain. Water races down riverbeds and channels and floods across the plains. Even when the rain stops, the water may take weeks to sink into the ground or dry up in the sun.

Spadefoot toad

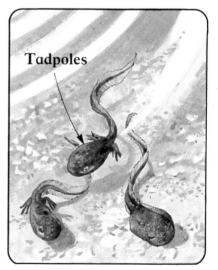

Tadpoles

After the rain, insects hatch and animals come out of their hiding places, like this toad.

It had buried itself to keep moist. Now it comes out to find a mate and lay eggs in the water.

The eggs hatch into tadpoles, which grow into toads before the pools of water dry up.

After the Rain

After the rain, green shoots push their way up out of the damp ground, and parts of the desert may be covered in a carpet of flowers.

They have grown from seeds that may have been lying there for many years. The seeds will not grow unless there is plenty of rain.

The flowers only bloom and live for a few weeks, while there is still enough water for them.

Insects come to drink nectar from them and spread pollen from one flower to another.

The flowers then make new seeds which drop to the ground and flower after the next rain.

Some plants can live in the desert all the year round because they store water.

Prickly pear cactus

Barrel cactus before rain

Barrel cactus after rain

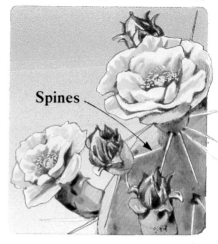

Spines

There are many kinds of cactus in America. They have tough skins but are juicy inside.

When it rains, their widespread roots soak up water and their stems swell to store it.

Cacti have flowers, but have spines, instead of leaves, to protect them from thirsty animals.

Saguaros

Cissus plant (Africa)

Welwitschia plant (Africa)

They grow very slowly, but some grow very tall. Cacti like this may be over 100 years old.

This shrub also stores water in its stem. Some desert trees store water in their trunks.

This plant collects dew on its leaves. Drops of water then drip to the ground above its roots.

Birds that live in the Desert

Desert birds all have special ways of living with the heat and shortage of water.

Ostrich

Flocks of budgerigars live in the Australian Outback. They drink at waterholes.

If it does not rain for a long time and the waterholes dry up, thousands of them die.

Sand grouse

The ostrich can go for days without drinking. It breathes fast to help it keep cool.

Birds that eat seeds must drink every day. The sand grouse flies a long way to find water.

It wets its breast feathers and flies back to its chicks, who suck the water from them.

Vultures

Vultures keep cool by soaring high in the sky. Their sharp eyes can spot a dead animal to eat from many miles away. When they see one, they swoop down to feed. They get the liquid they need from their prey's blood. Small birds get liquid by eating juicy insects.

Birds must shield their eggs from the sun. The Gila woodpecker builds its nest in a cactus.

When it leaves the hole it has made, another bird, such as this owl, moves in.

The burrowing owl makes its nest in a burrow that a prairie dog once lived in.

Surviving in the Desert

Deserts are so hot in the daytime that most animals would die if they stayed in the sun for long.

Most desert animals, like these American ones, seek shelter from the sun during the hottest part of the day

A bobcat dozes in the shade o a bush or rock, panting to hel keep cool. It goes hunting at night, when the desert is cool

Saguaro cactus

The American desert tortoise sometimes burrows underground to hide from the sun.

Horned lizard partly buried in the sand.

Coral snake

Reptiles, such as snakes and lizards, have tough leathery skins to protect them, but even they look for shade when it is hot.

Desert animals must be able to live without much water. Most of them get the liquid they need from the plants or insects they eat.

Jack rabbit

The jack rabbit's huge ears help it to keep cool, as well as to hear enemies coming.

Addax antelope

The addax antelope lives in the Sahara. It does not drink any water at all.

Camels can go without water for weeks, but then they drink gallons at a time.

Sidewinder rattlesnake

This rattlesnake has buried itself in the sand to keep cool, and to lie in wait for victims.

Kangaroo rats

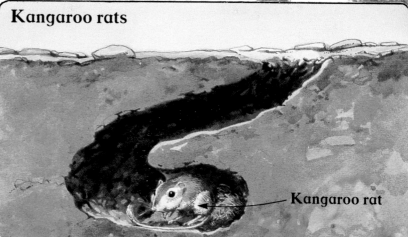

Kangaroo rat

The kangaroo rat digs a shallow burrow where it can hide and sleep during the day.

It does not drink any water. It gets all the moisture it needs from the seeds it eats.

Hunters and the Hunted

Most desert animals hunt at night. The kit fox's sand-colored fur is good camouflage.

It hunts kangaroo rats. They jump high, kicking sand in the fox's face, then run away.

Some lizards, like this Australian one, have a spiny skin to protect them from enemies.

How a rattlesnake hunts

Kangaroo rat

The rattlesnake is poisonous, but it will not attack large animals unless it is frightened. It shakes the rattle on its tail as a warning.

At night, when it is hunting, the snake is quiet. Small pits near its eyes and its forked tongue help it to sense when a small animal is near.

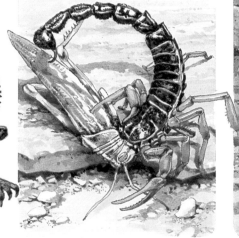

When this Australian lizard is in danger, it puffs out its frill to frighten its attacker.

The scorpion kills insects with the poisonous stinger at the end of its tail.

The trapdoor spider makes traps for insects. When insects fall in, the spider eats them.

The snake glides silently forward, then it quickly strikes. It sinks its poisonous fangs into its prey and then it lets go.

The animal runs away but dies very quickly. The snake goes after it. When it finds the dead animal, it swallows it whole.

Living in the Desert – 1

Living in the desert is difficult because water and food are hard to find. Many desert people are nomads and move from place to place.

The Tuaregs are nomads who live in the Sahara. They are herdsmen and travel from well to well, looking for pastures for their animals.

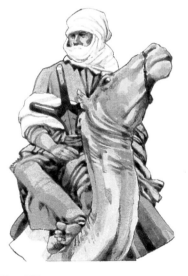

The Tuaregs were once fierce warriors who led great camel raids. They do not fight now.

They wear loose robes, to keep cool. They hang charms around their necks to ward off evil.

Tuareg men keep their faces veiled. The veil, called a tagilmust, is almost 20 feet long.

The Tuaregs keep camels, goats and sheep. They always camp near a well or waterhole, where the animals can drink and graze.

The women or children fetch water for the camp. They carry it in goatskin containers, which they sling under their mules.

Belongings in tree, out of reach of animals

Animals

Water container hanging from trestle

Tuaregs live in tents, which they carry with them. The tents are usually made of goatskins stitched together and stretched over poles.

The women collect firewood and cook the food. Here one woman is making bread while the other grinds corn to make a kind of flour.

Living in the Desert – 2

Not all nomads are like the Tuaregs. The San people of the Kalahari Desert do not keep herds, but collect plants to eat and hunt animals.

They wander from place to place, making grass huts to sleep in at night. Their way of life has not changed for thousands of years.

Every day the women look for roots to eat. They can spot plants even in the driest ground, and then dig them up with sharp sticks.

The men go hunting, using spears and poisoned arrows. There are few animals in the Kalahari and the hunters must track them down.

Empty ostrich egg

The San know how to find water under the ground. They suck it up through hollow reeds.

Sometimes they store water in buried ostrich egg shells, so that they can drink it later.

Australian Aborigines used to live like the San people, but now most of them live in towns.

When there is a long drought, the waterholes dry up and some nomads move to towns.

Many nomads are now learning to read and write, so they can get jobs if they desire.

More and more men who were nomads get jobs on farms or work in mines to earn a living.

A Sahara Salt Caravan

Some goods are still taken across the desert by caravans of camels. This Tuareg is packing salt to take across the Sahara and sell.

Camels are loaded with the heavy bundles. They can travel for several days without any water but they are sometimes bad-tempered.

The camels are tied together so they follow the leader and cannot run away. The men ride them when the sand is too hot to walk on.

The Tuaregs do not use maps to cross the desert. Instead they use the sun and stars as well as familiar landmarks to guide them.

Camels are hard to learn to ride.
They sway back and forth and from
side to side. Tuaregs steer them with
their feet and a rope.

Camels must drink every few days
when they are carrying heavy loads.
Tuaregs can sometimes find water
under the sand between the wells.

When there is a sandstorm, it is
impossible to travel. The caravan has
to stop and the men seek shelter from
the sand until the storm is over.

The caravan stops at night and the
men sit around a fire drinking tea
and telling stories. They sleep
wrapped in blankets on the ground.

Oases

An oasis is a place in the desert where there is water. The water comes from a spring or river. In an oasis trees and plants can grow.

Most oases, like this one in Tunisia, have towns built around them. Peopl can live here because there is always a supply of water.

People grow fruit trees and vegetables. Date palms grow easily and are useful for food and wood. This man is cutting dates.

There are two kinds of markets in Tunisian oasis towns. This is a food market. The food is piled up on woven mats on the ground.

A covered market is called a souk. Here most things are sold apart from food. Caravans bring goods from across the desert to these markets.

Houses in an oasis are usually made of mud or plaster. Their thick walls, flat roofs and small windows help to keep them cool inside.

Underground homes

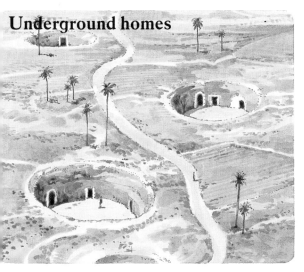

Some desert people live in very strange places. The Matmatans of Tunisia build their houses under the ground, where it is cooler.

Homes in the rocks

On the edge of the desert, in Turkey, people build houses in these rocks. They hollow out the insides and put in windows and doors.

Strange Sights in the Desert

Mirage

Thirsty travelers crossing deserts sometimes think they can see a lake in front of them. But as they move closer, the water disappears.

It is a trick of the light called a mirage. Hot air above the ground acts like a mirror. It reflects the sky and looks like water on the ground.

This is also a mirage. These camels are on dry land, but they look as if they are walking in water and we can see their reflections.

Sometimes dark clouds form and it looks as if it is starting to rain, but the hot air dries up the rain before it reaches the ground.

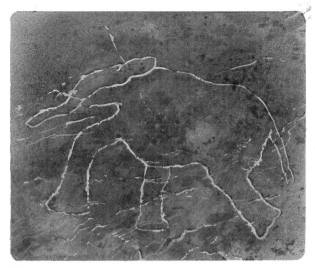

In some deserts, there are strange tree trunks made of stone. They are fossils of trees that grew in forests here 100 million years ago.

Deserts were not always as dry as they are now. Cave paintings in the Sahara show that animals, such as elephants, once roamed there.

In some places, there are ruins of old cities. There was once an oasis here, but the water dried up and the people had to move away.

This plain was once a lake. As the water began to dry up, it got saltier. Then it dried up completely and left a desert covered with salt.

Things that come from the Desert

Deserts are important for many reasons. They are the homes of people and animals, but they also provide materials such as diamonds and oil.

Oil well in the Arabian Desert

Oil and natural gas have been found under the Arabian, Sahara, American and Australian deserts. Scientists are always searching for more.

In Australia, uranium, nickel and alumina (to make into aluminum) are mined. Australia mines more alumina than any other country.

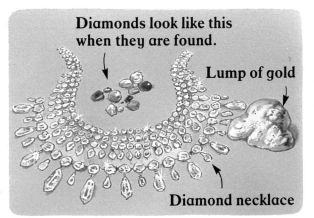

Diamonds look like this when they are found.

Lump of gold

Diamond necklace

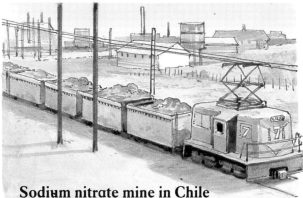

Sodium nitrate mine in Chile

Gold and diamonds have been found under the deserts in Australia, Namibia and South Africa. South Africa produces the most.

The Atacama Desert in Chile is the driest in the world, but has a lot of sodium nitrate. This is used to make fertilizers which help plants grow.

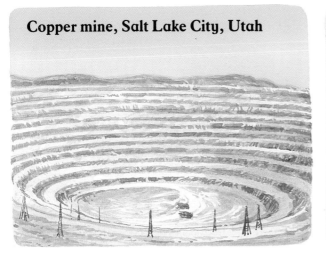

Copper mine, Salt Lake City, Utah

Many desert people now travel by car but still keep camels.

Chile also produces more copper than any other country. There are copper mines in the deserts of Australia, America and Mexico, too.

These discoveries mean that some desert countries have become richer. They have built roads, railways, airports and towns in the desert.

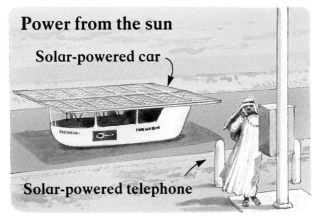

Power from the sun

Solar-powered car

Solar-powered telephone

Solar power station in the Mojave Desert, California, US

Scientists have found ways of changing the sun's heat into power to run things. This is called solar power. It is very useful in deserts.

The biggest solar power station is in the Mojave Desert where there are more than 300 sunny days each year. It cost 142 million dollars to build.

Making things grow in the Desert

Parts of some deserts are becoming even barer. People chop down trees for firewood, and their animals eat all the plants.

In some places, steady winds blow from one direction. If the wind brings sand toward an oasis, dunes build up, burying houses and trees.

Now people are trying to grow crops in the desert. In Iran, they spray oil on to sand dunes. This dries to a kind of thick crust.

Trees are planted in it and are protected from animals. When they grow, they help to keep the sand in place and make the soil richer.

Rivers flowing through deserts are dammed. Water can then be chaneled to nearby land and used to grow fruit and vegetables.

In Israel, plants are grown in plastic tents. When the plants are watered, the plastic stops the water from drying up in the hot sun.

The Imperial Valley in California used to be part of a big desert. Now fruit and vegetables are grown here all the year round.

To make the valley green, a canal was built to bring water from the Colorado river, almost 80 miles away. It is piped to all the fields.

Desert Locations

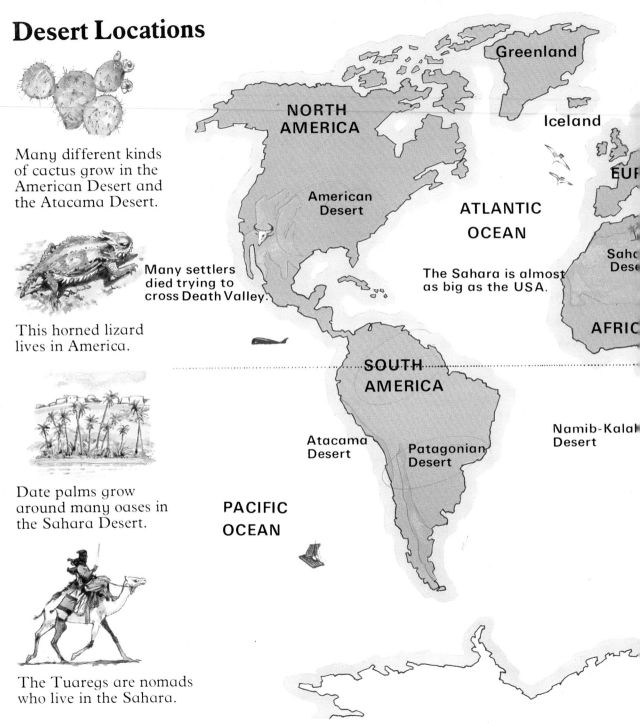

Many different kinds of cactus grow in the American Desert and the Atacama Desert.

This horned lizard lives in America.

Date palms grow around many oases in the Sahara Desert.

The Tuaregs are nomads who live in the Sahara.

Greenland

NORTH AMERICA

Iceland

EUR

American Desert

ATLANTIC OCEAN

Many settlers died trying to cross Death Valley.

The Sahara is almost as big as the USA.

Sah Des

AFRIC

SOUTH AMERICA

Atacama Desert

Patagonian Desert

Namib-Kalab Desert

PACIFIC OCEAN

Russia

ASIA

The Turkestan is
a cold, rocky desert.

Turkestan
Desert

Gobi
Desert

Negev
Desert

Iranian Desert

Arabian
Desert

Thar Desert

China

India

There is
a lot of oil
in the
Arabian Desert.

Equator

PACIFIC
OCEAN

INDIAN
OCEAN

Australian
Outback

Ayers
Rock

Aborigines believe
Ayers Rock is
a holy place.

Zealand

ANTARCTICA

The camels that live
in cold deserts, like
the Gobi, have two
humps and thick fur.

Welwitschia plants
grow in the Namib
Desert.

The San people live
in the Kalahari Desert.

Flocks of budgerigars
live in the dry
Australian Outback.

31

Index